CONFIDENCE FOR WOMEN

YOUR 12 STEP PLAN FOR TOTAL CONFIDENCE
AS A WOMAN MAKING YOUR OWN WAY

TABLE OF CONTENTS

ABOUT THIS BOOK

We see confidence as a practice. No two women are the same, yet all have the same ticking parts. This course is intended to shift the way you see yourself and the role that you as a woman play in this life. Essentially, it aims at rebuilding or strengthening your self-confidence level to a point where you can understand that your existence is not in vain, that you have a greater task here on earth than you ever thought possible, and that the possibilities are endless. It strives to teach you that you have to accept who you are now, take what you need from who you were yesterday and build each and every day towards who you want to be tomorrow.

In practice there isn't really one single book or guide that gives you definite answers as to how you should go about building your confidence as a woman living in the modern day world. We've drawn together a mass of enlightening resources to bring you the most comprehensive guide to use on this epic journey of rediscovering happiness and inevitably regaining your confidence.

This workshop focusses on helping you bring back happiness into your life in 12 easy-to-follow steps. 12 minutes a day for 12 days and you'll be on your way to becoming the best version of yourself.

FOREWORD

Dear reader,

I wish to congratulate you for making this investment in yourself, for having an open mind, and for being willing to *educate* yourself about how YOU can get the most out of your life.

If you are reading these lines, you truly are a rare and special person indeed, and I feel privileged to have the opportunity to reach you through this e-book.

Let me start off by saying that absolutely **anyone** can become totally self-confident.

All you have to do is model what confident people say, do, believe, and focus on.

It is an absolute fact that the most successful and self-confident people in the world today overcame the same self-doubt and feelings of inadequacy that plague the majority of us.

What you need to do to achieve Total Self-Confidence is simple and straightforward. If you put my suggestions into practice you *will* have a brand new life by the end of this 12 step program.

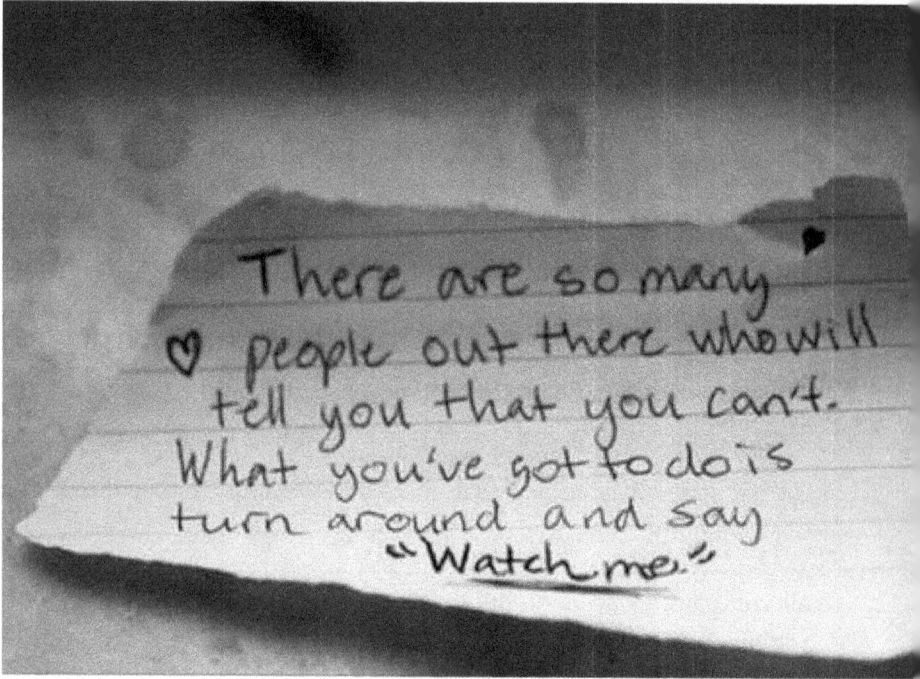

There are so many
♡ people out there who will
tell you that you can't.
What you've got to do is
turn around and say
"Watch me."

GIRLS SAY THEY FEEL: PRESSURED. BULLIED. UNSURE OF THEIR BODIES**.

WANTED
CONFIDENT GIRLS

ACCORDING TO A SURVEY* OF OVER 2,000 U.S. ADULTS OVER AGE 18

BULLIES are biggest threat to **GIRLS'** positive self-image.
followed by DRUG AND ALCOHOL USE and others

SO WHAT ELSE IS THERE

74% UNREALISTIC IMAGES of women in the media

69% inappropriate **SOCIAL MEDIA** use

74% POOR RELATIONSHIPS with parents

YEP, THE MEDIA

4 OUT OF 5 women say unrealistic images of women in the media are threat to girls' positive self-image

SEARCH

POST

YOU SHARED WHAT?
69% of adults think inappropriate photos/text messages threaten a girl's positive self-image

45% say a **positive role model** is THE BIGGEST asset to a young girl's development of a **healthy** self-image.

1 in 5 think **FRIENDSHIP SKILLS** or **GOAL SETTING** are biggest assets to a girl's self-image

WE ■👍Like

FIRST LADY MICHELLE OBAMA is top Role Model for girls
of those listed. (1 out of 2 adults)

BEST FOR GIRLS' SELF-IMAGE
45% Positive Role Models
Healthy Friendships **18%**
18% Goal Setting

42% Olympic gymnast Gabby Douglas

41% Oprah

36% Supreme Court Justice Sonia Sotomayor

23% Marissa Mayer
16% Sheryl Sandberg
10% Mary Kate and Ashley Olsen

Men are more likely than women to name business execs **Marissa Mayer** and **Sheryl Sandberg** as role models for girls.

HUH. REALLY? 4% of young adults (ages 18-34) picked Miley Cyrus as a role model for young girls

GENaustin
GIRLS EMPOWERMENT NETWORK

INTRODUCTION

My intention is to have you actually PUT INTO PRACTICE what you'll learn here, and GET CONCRETE RESULTS that will massively increase the quality of your life.

The key to this workshop is *action*. It is ACTION that will produce the results. Not just *"thinking about it..."* or going *"Wow, this sounds so interesting!"*

That is why you will have exercises to complete. I cannot emphasize enough how ***critical*** it is that you complete them! You will not get even a fraction of this workshop's value unless you ***do*** what is recommended here.

This workshop contains the best and most effective techniques and information on raising one's self-esteem and self-confidence. The reason it is concise is because YOU get to fill in the gaps. I don't want to fill your head with dozens of theories and bits of knowledge if they will produce zero results in your life. **So... _DO THE EXERCISES!_**

WHAT YOU CAN EXPECT FROM THIS COURSE

The essential aim of this workshop is for you to gain an absolute, irrepressible confidence in yourself as a woman that will make your life a joyful experience where everything just works. You should have the confidence to free yourself from fears and self-imposed limitations, pursue your dreams, live your purpose and make a difference in the world.

You need to understand that being shy and uncertain of yourself, just like being a strong and confident woman, is a choice you make every single day. It's all in the way you act; the behavioural pattern you choose to follow. Being totally self-confident is a learnt behavioural trait and one that anybody can learn to do. Practice makes perfect.

Eventually you'll be able to make being totally self-confident the way you choose to live every day. It will become part of your being.

WHY DO WE AS WOMEN NEED SELF-CONFIDENCE?

This course touches on one of the most important aspect of a woman's life – how she feels about herself.

You ARE how you feel about yourself!

Accepting who you are and loving what makes you unique is the single most important factor for experiencing joy, happiness and overall success in life.

When you come to love yourself and those around you, truthfully and without bounds, you'll discover how incredible this journey called life can really be, and that no matter what curve balls get thrown your way you can always find paradise in everyday situations.

You MUST love yourself completely.

This determines your STANDARDS for what you are willing to accept or settle for.

It determines how well you treat your body and your health, how much money you feel you deserve to earn or feel you can make, your belief in whether you can achieve your goals, how much others respect you and how they treat you, and even whether people like you and want to be around you.

People love being around confident people. You see, confident people do not feel the need to judge you or tear you down in order to elevate their own self-worth. They radiate a positive energy. You feel safe around them.

You need to consistently and confidently take action to move towards your goals, and towards your ultimate destiny.

People who lack in confidence often get 'stuck'. So you see, your entire DESTINY is shaped by your degree of confidence.

DEFINING SELF CONFIDENCE

True self-confidence comes from an absolute sense of certainty deep within that you are able to handle anything life throws your way.

Truly confident women exude calm, control, power, and certainty.

They care about people and they make people feel good when they are around them. They never brag – after all, actions speak louder than words. People who brag are just masking their insecurities.

People have varying degrees of confidence depending on what activity they are performing.

For example, someone might be totally confident in dressing up and putting their best foot forward, but feel totally inadequate at embarking on the journey of becoming a parent for the first time or starting out on a new job.

People with Total Self-Confidence, though, have complete belief in themselves.

They never ask themselves "Can I really do this? What if this doesn't work out? Am I good enough to pull it off?"

They know that if they really want something, and they are committed to getting it, it *will* happen.

They know that it's just a question of time until they've mastered the skills and knowledge to make whatever they want a reality.

You have a right to be self-confident and owe it to yourself to find that essence.

We are born fearless and completely uninhibited, feeling no pressure to conform.

Kids are totally empowered, and self-confident. They only do what they *enjoy* doing... or they don't participate! What a concept!

They live in the 'now', are joyful, playful, and thoroughly dig into life! They live in constant wonder and amazement, willing to explore everything, with no fear of the unknown!

All other fears we had to learn from our parents and our environment. They are *inauthentic* fears. They do not really exist outside of our heads. You can learn to put all those fears back where they belong – the dustbin.

What would happen in *your* life if you were to adopt a child-like belief in yourself?

Babies keep trying to walk until they *can* walk. They have to fall over again and again and again in the process, but they keep getting up and trying again!

Most adults are afraid to even *try* something new in case they fail! And if they *do* 'fail' the first time around, they never try that thing again, because it doesn't make them 'look good'!

Can you imagine if a baby were to say, "Nope, walking isn't for me – tried it once, it's really not all that it's cracked up to be...?"

All those fears are *learnt* behaviors – layers upon layers of *nonsense* that most people have accepted as real. They are but an illusion that exist nowhere other than in your head!

The truth: anything and everything is available to us.

You see, most women explain away their perceived 'failures' or lack of success by saying things like, "This can't be done," "Be realistic," "It wasn't meant to be," "I'm too old to do this…," or "You gotta pay the bills…"

When you give up on your dreams, you are killing off your *soul*! Most people are dead at 30, buried at 70! Is *that* what *you* want for your life? What are *your* big dreams?

It is tragic how we have been culturally indoctrinated and socially conditioned to stop believing in our dreams and instead strive to fit into a tiny little box of what is expected of us… *Go to school… get a job… get a mortgage… get a husband.*

Surely there is *more* to life, isn't there?

Deep down, you know these words ring true – they resonate with your true self.

WHERE DID I LOSE MY SELF CONFIDENCE?

The simple answer? You MADE that decision.

You <u>decided</u> you weren't 'good' or that 'I can't do this', 'I can't have that', 'there's something wrong with me'…

If a child's parents lack in self-confidence and self-esteem, it is almost guaranteed that the child will grow up with exactly <u>the same</u> learned behaviours.

Monkey see, monkey do…

Another source of lack of confidence is being reprimanded for making mistakes.

As a young child, as you're discovering the world and learning literally millions of new things, how many chances are there for you to get things wrong?

LOADS!!! You get to make thousands of mistakes again and again!

That's how people learn! From trying things and making mistakes!

When a woman gives birth to a child, her body is flushed with Oxytocin, a powerful chemical that quietens the judgemental mind and makes her feel unconditional love. The effects of this chemical wears off after approximately 18 months to 2 years.

So for the first couple of years, whatever the child does, whether it pees everywhere, smashes the furniture, or keeps you awake night after night… it's fine, the mother does not get upset. She loves the child unconditionally. It means *"I love you no matter what"*. She loves the child without imposing the condition *"I will love you IF you act like a good boy/girl"*, whatever *'good'* might mean in this particular instance.

Now, a couple of years on, with the effect of Oxytocin wearing off, the child might accidentally break something, and this time, instead of accepting this as normal, what often happens is that parents lash out at the child, screaming something to the effect of, *"Bad boy! Why did you do that? Don't do that AGAIN! You can't do that!"*

Now, if you hear, *"You can't do that"* enough times… do you think that as an adult you feel like "Anything Is Possible"?

Or do you, instead, shut off millions of possibilities that would otherwise be open to you?

If we are punished as children for exploring our environment, we develop a fear of the new. Many of us are terrified of making mistakes as a result of this type of punishment. We stay in our comfort zone to avoid the fear of failure and rationalize our decision.

In this first moment of 'abuse', something crucial and utterly destructive happens in a child's mind.

Fear sets in.

"Mommy and daddy don't love me. I'm going to be left all alone."

Fear of rejection has many people focusing unhealthily on the opinions and thoughts of others. Some can't do or say anything without fearing the disapproval of others.

They live lives far below their potential and their reactions to the tiniest disagreement are blown totally out of proportion.

It's easy to see why most people are afraid to tell the truth or confront someone truthfully. If we fear failure, feel unworthy or fear rejection, we won't confront another because of our fear of being wrong, of making a mistake, of being disliked or of our own problems being brought into the open.

Our need for love and connection is more powerful than most people give it credit. I dare say it is the reason behind almost everything we do...

Quickly, the child learns how to act in order to please its parents, how to *manipulate* his way into getting what is now *conditional* love.

The parents love him IF he conforms to their rules. The child is loved as long as it does what is expected of it.

The child learns to conform, to suppress its natural instincts and desires, to avoid doing things it enjoys, etc.

Now, what do you think having someone say to you again and again, at such a young age, *"DON'T do this! You CAN'T do that!"*... does to a child's mind?

When you are used to unconditional love, and suddenly someone screams at you for "doing something wrong", do you think that maybe in a confused 2-year-old's mind the idea *"There's something wrong with me...."* could set in?

Then, a few years later, it's time to go to school.

Again, LOADS of occasions to make errors, mistakes, and get it wrong, when there are others that seem to get it *'right'*.

What does a young child's mind decide then?

"I'm not good enough".

By the time adolescence comes around, this belief often has expanded to *"I'm no good at ALL!"* As a teenager you get occasion after occasion to feel *"not good enough"*.

The media feed you an image of how you *should* be and peer pressure makes you want to conform to fit in and be 'cool' ... so as to not lose that love/connection with others.

Soon you feel that you're not rich enough, not smart enough, not pretty enough, not good-smelling enough...that you don't have a good enough body or a good enough relationship...

Most people have learnt how to survive inside of *"There's something wrong with me"* – a belief they created when they were 2-3 years old!!!

You have designed your life to succeed in order to survive *"There's something wrong with me"*. It's all about covering up *"There's something wrong with me"*. You hope you fake it long enough so that no one ever finds out...

You try all the time to hide this from other people. 99% of what you do is about "Looking Good".

The funny bit is... EVERYONE ELSE OUT THERE IS TERRIFIED OF WHAT <u>YOU</u> THINK OF <u>THEM</u>!

THE MEDIA AND THEIR EFFECT ON YOUR SELF CONFIDENCE

Pick up any magazine, turn on any TV channel, and you'll be bombarded with ad after ad after ad of gorgeous young super-models and the lifestyles of ultra-wealthy individuals.

Now, I don't know about you, but all that doesn't exactly make me feel great about *my* lifestyle or the way *I* look...

As you can imagine, individuality, independent thinking, and self-confidence in ourselves and our choices is the *last* thing they want! They want you to buy things to *conform* and *"Keep up with the Joneses"*! They most definitely *don't* want you thinking for yourself of whether their products are right for you or not! They want you to feel *frightened* into purchasing things, and they want you to feel *bad* if you *don't* have what – allegedly – everyone else has!

RECAP

By this stage you feel unworthy because you upset your parents when you were 2 years old, or because of your parents' issues and problems, and because you didn't answer some questions correctly at school when you were 6, and because you felt like you didn't fit into an image of how you *should* be as defined by an industry that survives on instilling fear into you so that you buy more products...

Your life is absurd! It makes no sense whatsoever!

The TRUTH: who you are is *ANYTHING IS POSSIBLE*!

You are here to live and experience everything, AND PLAY FULL OUT! You are here to pursue your dreams and live out your purpose with PASSION!

MILLENNIAL WOMEN
REDEFINE AMBITION IN THE WORKPLACE

Nearly 50% Say The Sacrifices For Women Leaders Aren't Worth It
A survey of 1,000 Canadian Millennial women revealed that women are charting their own career paths and they don't all involve aspiring to the top ranks.

DIVERSE AMBITION

38% WANT great, rewarding, interesting work but don't care about leading others

18 PERCENT want to be the #1 le of a large or promi organization or sta

Almost one-in-ten care about being a cre person working on their own or on a s team of like-minded people

TOP CAREER ROAD B

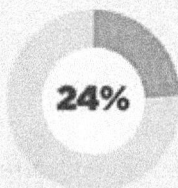

24%
Inability to balance professional goals with being a parent

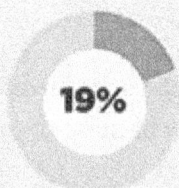

19%
Lack of self-confidence

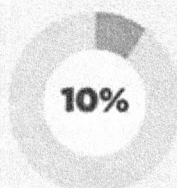

10%
Lack of role models or mentors

10%
Lack of sk educati

BALANCING ACT

74% of Millennial women are concerned abo acheiving the right balance between person professional goals

87%
Agree that female leaders have to make more sacrifices than male leaders

84%
Believe they can juggle work and family life over the long haul

54%
Willing to sacrifice aspects of their personal life to achieve professional goals

42%
Agree that sacrifices fe leaders hav make aren't v

MILLENNIAL WORKING N

LESS THAN 1/4 OF WORKING MOMS aspire to be the #1 leader of a large or prominent organization or start-up

86% OF WORKING MOMS are on track to achieving their professional goal

91 PERCENT Say they ca juggle worl and family

CONFIDENCE FOR WOMEN

12 MINUTES FOR SELF ANALYSING THE WOMAN IN YOU

The first step for you as a woman to regain self-confidence is (simple as it may sound) to buy a journal.

In this journal you are going to figure out who you are and what your life purpose is. You'll be analyzing your behavioral traits and finding ways to regain happiness in life.

What this journal will contain is thoughts about everything in your life that you want to change, everything you no longer want written as part of your life story and everything you want to include in your new life, a.k.a. your goals.

What you'll learn from this is that all that you are is essentially a result of what you have thought. You'll see that the fears and beliefs you keep your true self locked up with are completely disempowering and illogical.

Your very first exercise on the path to regaining your self-confidence starts here. In your journal write down the answer to these questions. Remember that this is all about you so be completely honest with yourself.

EXERCISE 1

1. What is there in your life that you are not happy about? What can you do to change this?

2. What are 2 realities about yourself that you find difficult to accept completely?

3. When do you feel the most angry or frustrated? What is it about those situations that make you feel that way?

4. List 5 fears you currently hold. What do you fear most in your life right now? Why? What would it mean if that happened?

Complete the following beginnings:

'I like myself least when I...'

'I like myself most when I...'

RECAP

By now you should have some understanding of what you do and don't like about yourself, what makes you tick and what your game plan is going to be from here on out.

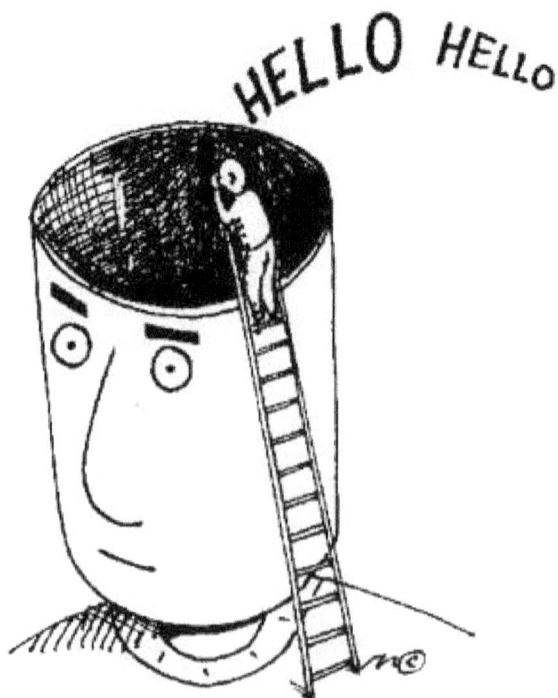

12 MINUTES FOR TOTAL HONESTY

ADMITTING YOUR FLAWS

If there is something in your life or something about yourself that you are unhappy about, in order for it to go away, as simple as this may sound, the first step is to KNOW that it exists!

The first step to solving a problem… is admitting you *have* one!

Don't practice self-delusion – face it as it is, not as you wish it to be. Be completely honest with yourself. Don't pretend like the problem is not there. See it as it is.

If there's a 'problem'…JUST FACE IT STRAIGHT ON! GET IT HANDLED! THEN MOVE ON. Don't ever stay in a situation that makes you unhappy or that you feel is wrong for you in any way. Visualize your desired outcome, and TAKE ACTION to make it as you want it to be.

No one is perfect and even though we hear it all too often, some of us still refuse to take it to heart.

Self-assured women don't only admit their imperfections, but they applaud them. The flaws in you are a part of who you are. They point out where your strengths lie, shows you where you need to improve and when to let others take the lead. Trying to be perfect at everything you do is unrealistic. The game never gets easier, you just get better at it. Love yourself for who you are and who you know you're not.

OWNING YOUR FEELINGS

All that exists in your life, good or bad, is there because of **YOUR** attitudes, beliefs, thoughts, choices, and actions.

You and you alone have 'manifested' these situations. You have attracted these situations and people into your life, through your way of 'being' and through your dominant thoughts.

Regardless of the situation, confident women strive to understand their emotions and own up to them. Self-assured women seize the opportunity for self-expression without the need to blame others. They say how they feel when they feel it and make sure others understand what they just said.

Make your feelings your own, understand them and have the freedom to express them whenever they need to be spilled to listening ears.

RELEASING YOUR GUILT

What was originally supposed to be just a temporary emotion has more than half the women of the world riding on an emotional rollercoaster. Guilt was a tool designed to make us question our actions, act to correct our mistakes and then apologize if it was necessary. But that's all it was ever intended to be.

Guilt is not meant to break down our emotional foundations. Confident women listen to their guilt feelings, map out how to make right what they did wrong and then they let it go.

If you're feeling guilty about something, take a moment to name that feeling, person or event that caused you to feel that way. Try to figure out how you can make the wrong that you did be right again, and then move on with your life. At least then you can say that from your side you tried, and we mean, really tried.

LETTING GO OF YOUR PAST

Other than in your head, your past is something that does not exist.

Forgive yourself for your past mistakes! We're all are going to screw up at some time! You may have made poor choices – acknowledge them, learn from them, forgive yourself, and MOVE ON.

Let go of the past! Release it! Live in the <u>NOW</u>! Be excited about the <u>FUTURE</u>! Embrace who you are. Accept who you are. Love your SELF.

There are steps you must follow to rid yourself of past guilt you may be holding onto. They are as follows:

1. Accept your responsibility for the action. Do not deny it. Own it.

2. Explore the reasons you had at the time for behaving as you did. By understanding ourselves we stop repeating the mistakes. If we merely condemn ourselves, our behaviour tends to get worse along with our self-esteem.

3. If our action has hurt others and it's possible to communicate with them, let those hurt know you acknowledge the consequences of your behaviour.

4. Do anything and everything possible to minimise the harm you've caused, e.g. return something stolen, fix something broken, apologise where harsh words were spoken, tell the truth where you previously lied, etc.

EXERCISE II

1. Who has wronged you in the past?

2. Whom have *you* wronged in the past?

3. With whom do you need to "complete" with so that neither of you carry this issue around anymore?

Make a list.

Write these people a letter explaining what was going on for you, and how you feel about it now. You don't *need* to be apologetic – although people are bowled over when someone has the courage and self-esteem to admit they were wrong – you can simply acknowledge what happened for you.

Contact them by phone and read the letter out to them.

I know it sounds tough, but what is the cost of *not* doing this? Do you really want to go through life accumulating all this garbage that is weighing you down? Every time we leave something incomplete, it's like taking on us one more bag of dirty laundry...

You will see that clearing the past and completing with the past will give you an unbelievable sense of freedom and power.

Forgiveness is a vital factor in moving on from the pain of the past. Forgive who you need to forgive. **Not only must we forgive others for perceived wrongs, but we must learn how to forgive ourselves also.**

Most of us are much too hard on ourselves and need to remember that we always do our best. We always do the most we can, as we know it, at any given time to achieve happiness.

Forgiveness is KEY for a quality life!

RECAP

By now you should have admitted to the "not so awesome" qualities of yourself but in the same sense have the guts to accept them as a part of who you are in essence.

You should have worked on how you feel about negative events in your life and figured out what made you feel that way. You should also be in the process of letting go of the guilt about past experiences that you obviously cannot change at this point.

You are going to do Exercise II where you will figure out who you have wronged, write a letter to that person and then give them a ring to read the letter to them. Don't say sorry if you aren't feeling it, but just fess up and get it off your chest.

> **"To design the future effectively, you must first let go of your past."**
>
> Charles J. Givens

12 MINUTES FOR BUIDING YOUR DREAM

In order to create a life where you are a totally self-confident woman you need to be able to set your own goals in order to build an outcome that you are happy with.

Confident people know what they want. They are goal-oriented.

Goals work because **thoughts are things**. Everything you see around you was first created in someone's imagination. Whatever we imagine and focus on we move towards, and we then create and manifest.

Also, you are acknowledging to both your conscious & subconscious mind that where you are right now is not where you want to be.

Dissatisfaction can be a tool to push you towards achieving your goals. You see, part of what motivates human action is a sense of dissatisfaction, and without a certain amount of pressure, there is no motivation.

THE POWER OF KNOWING YOUR OWN OUTCOME

A compelling goal can make you jump out of bed every day with amazing drive and energy! You need a long-term vision of what you want your life to be about, a compelling future that excites you and gets you going!

The power of writing down your goals is simply extraordinary. Quite simply, THEY WORK. If you write down your goals on a piece of paper, then carry them around with you or stick your goals all around your house, car, and office so that you see them frequently, **YOUR SUCCESS IS PRACTICALLY ASSURED.**

Know what you want. Know your outcome. Clarity is POWER!

Your brain is constantly screening out and deleting 99.9% of everything you perceive. You would go crazy with 'information overload' if it didn't!

Your Reticular Activating System (RAS) will bring to your attention that 0.01% that your brain feels is important.

The way you can get your RAS to work for you in an empowering way... is **by setting GOALS.**

When you write down a goal, you are in fact sending a clear order to your brain (and your RAS) that **THIS IS _IMPORTANT_, THIS IS WHAT I WANT, NOW GET IT FOR ME!**

EXERCISE III

OK, now grab a pen and some paper, and start answering the questions below.

1. If you had 100 million dollars in the bank and absolutely no limitations whatsoever, what would you be doing right now? Imagine that you were granted 1 wish – what would you dare to dream, if you knew you could not fail?

2. What kind of work would you truly enjoy and be passionate about? Are you currently doing the type of work you love to do? If not, what has stopped you so far from pursuing it? Do you plan to continue allowing that to stop you? If not, what could you do to change that?

3. If you had no limitations, where would you want to travel? What would you want to experience?

4. If you learnt today that you only had 6 months to live, what would you do with that remaining time? What is _really_ important to you? What do you want to leave behind?

5. What knowledge or skill would you like to acquire?

6. What do you want for your body and your health? Do you want to be healthy, fit, and vibrant?

7. What do you want to achieve financially? Do you want to earn $1 million? $100 million? Do you want to earn $10,000 a month? Do you want to eliminate all your debts? Do you have investment goals or savings targets for the next year, 5 years, 10 years, etc.?

8. What would you like buy? What toys, gadgets, or general items have you always wanted?

9. What specific characteristics do you want your ideal life partner to possess? Describe your ideal partner!

10. What would you like to contribute to the world?

11. What would you like to create?

12. What would your dream house look like? What would be in it?

13. Who are your heroes? Who would you like to be more like? What character traits would you like to develop?

Once you've got your list of goals, you'll need to review your goals daily. Stick them in your diary, on your fridge, in your car, on your computer, next to your bed, laminate them and stick them in the shower!

Whatever you focus on consistently you will get or become!

By the way, if you have a desire for something, that means YOU ALREADY HAVE THE ABILITY WITHIN YOU to achieve your desires. What you can *conceive*, you can *believe*, and therefore you can *achieve*. Period! Can you imagine what achieving your goals would do to your self-confidence?

What has *thinking* about your goals done for you already? Do you feel more in control of your life? Do you feel the power that comes from this simple act?

YOU ARE NOW DICTATING YOUR TERMS ON LIFE – IT'S YOU THAT DETERMINES HOW THINGS ARE GOING TO BE. YOU ARE IN CONTROL.

Next you have to decide (and stick to) the person you WANT TO BE.

You see, who you ARE is *way* more important than what you HAVE or what you are DOING.

EXERCISE IV-THE PERSON I WANT TO BE / MY CODE OF CONDUCT

Write down your own version of the list below. Who is your ideal self? Who were you born to be? Imagine they are writing your obituary – what would you like them to say about you?

-I am disciplined

-I possess total self-confidence and self-mastery

-I am patient and perseverant

-I am positive, enthusiastic, passionate, committed!

-I never speak negatively of anyone

-I always smile at everyone and I walk tall

-I take excellent care of my health

-I am direct, candid, and straight-forward

-I have no need for approval

-I am solution-oriented

-I never complain nor express anger

-I am a leader

-I never give up on my dreams

-I am brave and unreasonable

-I never procrastinate and instead do things NOW

-I accept full responsibility for my life

RECAP

After you have worked through this chapter you would have worked out a life script, specified in detail what it is that you want to do with your life, you are now in control.

You will have also written your code of conduct; your character definition to which you will stick from here on out.

12 MINUTES OF APPRECIATION AND THANKSGIVING

IDENTIFYING YOUR HEROES

What could help you really stick to your "code of conduct" is a list of your heroes, people you look up to.

You don't have to know these people personally. On the other hand, a hero could be someone you know very well, like your mother.

In my mind's eye, I have a boardroom where I regularly meet with these people who advise me about what I should do to make an even bigger difference in the world. In there, they are my peers and they value my contribution.

Who do YOU want to be like?

What would it do for your self-confidence and self-esteem if you were to act like your heroes and spend time with them?

Raise your standards. Imagine that your heroes become your peers. Imagine that you are a public figure –how would you act *then*?

EXERCISE V

Write a list of 6 of your heroes, and collate pictures of them on a sheet of paper that you will have somewhere you can see every day.

What you need to do from here is write down your "Life Script". Plan out (in the finest detail) how your life will be. For example "In 5 years' time I will be living in the house of my dreams with a big yard and my dogs and children will be running around playing while my husband and I admire all of our blessings".

EXERCISE VI

Now that you've written down your goals, Code of Conduct and your Life Script... VISUALIZE THEM! Play a mental movie in your head, and then see yourself getting into that movie!

Mentally rehearse it again and again and again! Absolutely EXPECT it to happen.

Make the picture big and bright! Put yourself in the picture! See your ideal self, smiling and being happy! What do you hear? What do you smell? What do you see? Who is around you?

Feel what you would feel if these goals were already yours! Get excited!

Create clear mental pictures of the person you want to be and the things you want to do. So clear you believe them 100%. Your subconscious can't tell the difference between reality and desire. The key to this exercise is the amount of emotion you instil your imagined picture with.

Your subconscious mind is 30,000 times more powerful than your conscious mind. You can tap into its extraordinary power through visualization. By concentrating on this visualization for 5 straight minutes, you are burning an imprint of it on your subconscious mind, and it will go to work immediately to bring to you anything and everything you desire.

RECAP

By the end of this chapter you should have identified your role models and have written down your Life Script (a detailed action plan as to how your life is going to go from here on out) and should be practising visualisations of the goals you have set for yourself. Practice makes perfect. Remember that. Commit to it every single day!

CONFIDENCE FOR WOMEN

S.M.A.R.T. Goal Setting for Success

12 MINUTES FOR POSITIVE AFFIRMATION

Who are you REALLY? Who *determines* who you are?

The answer...*YOU* do.

Most people let others define who they are.

The words that come out of your mouth to describe yourself will become you. As you describe yourself, so you are! Speak your empowering affirmations powerfully and with passion – send a clear message to your subconscious, *burn* that feeling into your subconscious!

EXERCISE VII

Choose from the list below some adjectives, a couple of nouns, and a verb, to form a sentence to describe yourself such as *"I am an Outstanding, Inspirational, and Charismatic Leader and Visionary, that Makes A Difference and Defies All Odds!"*

Outstanding	Leader	Achie
Magnetic	Visionary	Leads
Awesome	Role-model	Motiv
Sensual, sexy	Free spirit	Envisi
Inspirational, Charismatic	Guide	Chang
Confident	Teacher	Create
Phenomenal	Mentor	Gets r
Powerful, Strong	Legend	Makes
Invincible	Motivator	Comm
Irrepressible, Unstoppable	Champion	Inspire
Dynamic, Energetic	Force For Good	Discov
Unforgettable	Star!	Enligh
Honest, True	Achiever	Gives
Creative	Maker of dreams	Grows
Sensational, Sublime	Creator of Magic	Steps
Joyful, Alive!	Millionaire	Create
Passionate	Master	Rocks!
Impulsive, Spontaneous	Hero	Lives L
Warm, Natural	Philosopher	Laughs
Kind, Caring, Compassionate	Warrior	Takes
Fabulous, Stupendous!	Poet	Shines
Marvellous, Gorgeous	Icon	Transf
Fearless, Brave, Courageous	Firewalker!	Defies
Talented	Entertainer	Touche
Highly Intelligent	Innovator	Revolu

40

CONFIDENCE FOR WOMEN

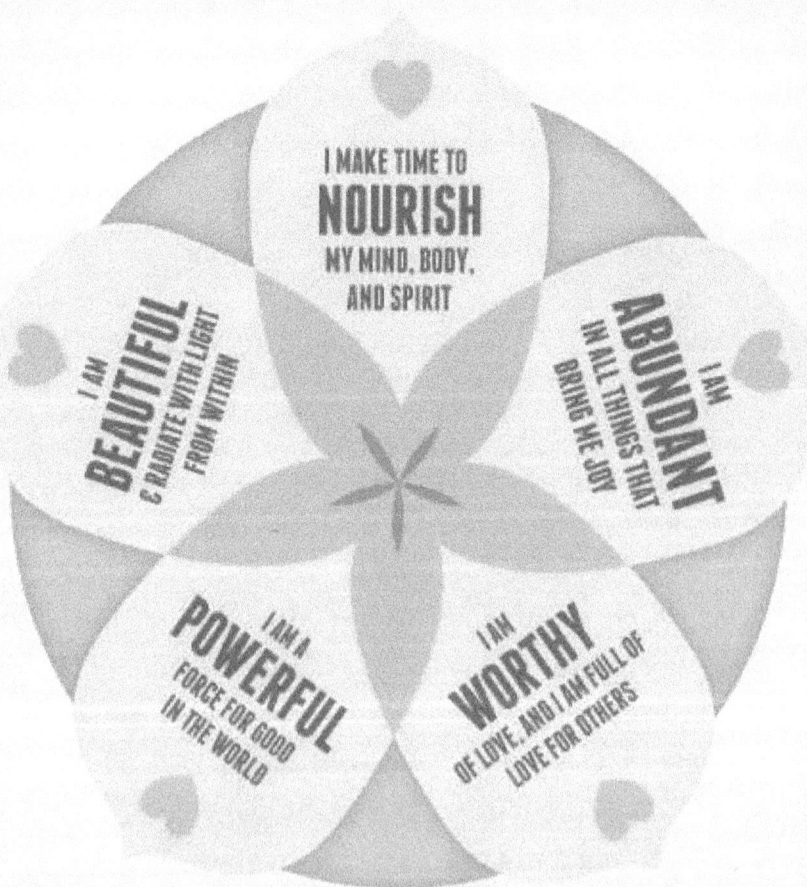

5 MANTRAS FOR DAILY SELF-LOVE

Repeat these kind & positive messages to yourself every day, & you'll greatly increase your level of health & happiness

I MAKE TIME TO **NOURISH** MY MIND, BODY, AND SPIRIT

I AM **BEAUTIFUL** & RADIATE WITH LIGHT FROM WITHIN

I AM **ABUNDANT** IN ALL THINGS THAT BRING ME JOY

I AM A **POWERFUL** FORCE FOR GOOD IN THE WORLD

I AM **WORTHY** OF LOVE, AND I AM FULL OF LOVE FOR OTHERS

12 MINUTES FOR DEVOTION AND DISCIPLINE

Set up a regime for the woman in you.

Discipline means doing things that are difficult or less than pleasant. It strengthens your character and self-control. It strengthens your will. Consequently, it massively strengthens your self-confidence.

Discipline is crucial when it comes to your health, taking care of your body, taking care of your finances... EVERYTHING!

If you *say* you're going to do something that you know is tough but that is good for you, and you do it again and again anyway... you will massively increase your esteem for yourself.

I have a list that I call my **"POWER REGIMEN"**.

It is my routine for the day.

It looks something like this:

-Get up at 05:30

-30 Minute morning workout

-Connect with Goals / Visualize / Incantation & Prayer / Gratitude

-Plan your day / KNOW YOUR OUTCOME

-Read/Learn 30 minutes

-Meditate 15 minutes

-Sleep at 00.00

Whenever you exert discipline and self-mastery you strengthen your self-confidence.

Make a promise to yourself and keep it for 10 days. See how it makes you feel, feel how much power this gives you.

Discipline is an act of LOVE! Demonstrate love for yourself! You are extremely important, so act this way! Look after your own body.

EXERCISE VIII

Write down your own "Power Regimen" – what are *you* committed to doing for yourself every day?

Commit to the cause. Every. Single. Day!

Integrity demands that you are STRAIGHT WITH YOURSELF.

Sometimes it's the toughest thing you'll ever have to do... but it's the foundation of a joyous life, self-expression, power... everything.

You don't say 'yes' to please people, or because it's the right thing to say, or because it makes you *"look good"*.

The foundation of self-confidence is living in accordance with your values.

As long as you know you're doing the right thing, the world can collapse around you and you'll maintain peace of mind, calm and confidence.

Integrity is vital to high self-confidence. It is an essential value to have, and it is more than a value, as it ensures that all your other values are respected and lived in line with.

You can't have *a little bit* of integrity; you can't put it aside when it's not convenient.

From the moment you've selected your values, you will never compromise them. This is the measure of your quality as a human being. As long as you know deep down that you'll never violate your highest value, you'll be in control and self-confident.

ARE <u>YOU</u> ACTUALLY HONOURING YOUR WORD WITH YOUR LIFE?

EXERCISE IX

What would you do differently if Integrity were your highest value? Where in your life are you "out of integrity"?

Resolve to get back into Integrity in all those areas within the next month.

RECAP

By the end of this chapter you should have designed an easy to follow, no excuses regime that you intend to follow every day in order to establish a devotional commitment towards achieving self-confidence. You have to be able to follow this EVERY SINGLE DAY in order to achieve maximum results.

12 MINUTES FOR BEING REAL

JUST SAY NO

This might sound a little like catty behaviour, but in reality it's actually pretty respectful. Confident women do not overcommit and they do not make false promises. The just say no if they really can't or don't want to do something.

Why?

Because they would rather state the truth and decline than to tell a white lie only to flake out later. And they don't have time for everything. To be honest, no one does. Burnouts definitely are not part of any confident woman's agenda, so she makes sure that she only commits to things she'll get around to doing, and essentially, wants to spend her time on. Truth bombs work. They don't hurt half as much as having to disappoint people after a commitment has already been made. So from here on out your motto should be to just SAY NO whenever you don't feel like doing something; plain and simple.

NEVER CAVE IN OR CONFORM

Confident women don't wear clothes, say things, listen to music, do things or become anything they don't believe in, because they aren't walking cookie cutters.

Confident women don't mirror others to find what makes them happy. They are brave enough to look within. They stand up for who they are and proudly announce themselves, never trying to just blend in with the crowd.

It's better to be hated for who you are than to be loved for something that you are not.

RECAP

By the end of this chapter you should know that you have the right (and owe it to yourself) to say NO when you feel like it and have the perseverance to not cave in and become just another copy of someone else. You should no longer budge to the "ideal" of what women should be, but instead be able to proudly strut your stuff.

12 MINUTES OF MEANINGFUL MIND CONTROL

All that we are is a result of what we have thought.

This might seem hard to believe, but your thoughts are the most powerful tool in the universe.

With your thoughts you create your world. Think about it. Everything you see around you started off in someone's imagination. It all began with a thought.

Your outer world is a mirror image of your inner world. Whatever you dwell on will manifest in your outer life. In fact, the *more* you dwell on something, the more it manifests. *Where your attention goes, energy flows.*

You attract into your life the people, the circumstances, and the opportunities that are in harmony with your dominant thoughts.

The average person has 70,000 thoughts a day, and 55,000 of them are negative. Is it any surprise most people manifest unhappiness and lack of success?

The only smart thing to do is to persistently think about your goals and have thoughts that are consistent with the person you'd like to be.

The more you think about these things, the more that image engraves itself into your subconscious mind and the latter will go to work, 24/7, to bring it into reality.

Now, since your mind can only hold one thought at a time, make sure these are positive thoughts!

Most people are plagued by self-doubt and insecurity because they dwell on their weaknesses, their fears, and their perceived 'failures'.

Realize that you and you alone control your thoughts. No one else.

You need to learn to control the focus of your mind!

How do you do that?

DECIDE to focus on your successes, your strengths, and your goals. Focus on what's going right in your life, what you are grateful for, and what you are proud about.

EXERCISE X

Write down your answers to the following questions and read your answers frequently every day, with *feeling*.

1. What are you *grateful* for in life?

2. What are you really *excited* about right now?

3. Who do you love and who really loves you?

RECAP

By the end of this chapter you should know how to focus your mind's power into envisioning the perfect state of self-confidence so that you can reflect it into your daily life.

You should have listed what you feel grateful for in life, what you are currently really excited about and who you love as well as who loves you.

ALL THAT WE ARE
IS THE RESULT OF
WHAT WE HAVE
THOUGHT. THE
MIND IS
EVERYTHING.
WHAT WE THINK
WE BECOME.

BUDDHA

QuotePixel.com

12 MINUTES FOR SEEING THINGS THE WAY THEY ARE

Experiences, events, or situations HAVE NO MEANING OTHER THAN THAT WHICH WE GIVE THEM.

'Meaning' is a purely subjective phenomenon. Objectively, it does not exist in reality.

You have a choice about what you make of anything that happens in your world.

Instead of being offended or hurt by an insult, ask yourself "What can I learn from this? What is going on in that person's life that makes them act this way?" Get curious!

The point here is *this*: what events have *you* blown totally out of proportion, that still affect you today? What *meaning* did you attach to them?

12 MINUTES FOR NOT CARING WHAT "THEY" THINK

This might come as a shock to you, but...

THERE ARE MORE IMPORTANT THINGS IN LIFE THAN WHAT OTHER PEOPLE THINK!

99% of what people do is about *"looking good"* and *"what other people think."*

Our choices of career, car, house, partner, university degree, hobbies, what we wear, who we hang out with, and where we go out are all influenced in this way.

We are TERRIFIED of what other people think about us!

What's hilarious about this is that 99% of people out there... are terrified of YOU and what YOU think of *THEM*!!! AND FURTHERMORE, THEY HAVE ZERO TIME TO THINK ABOUT YOU BECAUSE THEY ARE TOO WORRIED ABOUT WHAT OTHERS THINK ABOUT *THEM*!!!

You are much more powerful than you think – people are terrified that what *you* have to say about *them* could be hurtful...

Being FREE of the fear of "what other people think" is the most liberating experience you can imagine.

Imagine being able to be totally upfront with people. Imagine being able to tell someone, squarely, that their performance or that their actions are not up to scratch.

Not in a nasty, mean way, but simply asserting yourself, giving yourself the right to tell people the truth, without fearing that *they might not like you*.

What's weird is that, when you have the self-confidence to be upfront and honest with people, they will respect you immensely, even if they don't like what you have to tell them.

YOUR self-respect will increase dramatically as well.

Again, remember this crucial point: THERE ARE MORE IMPORTANT THINGS IN LIFE THAN WHAT OTHER PEOPLE THINK!

RECAP

By the end of the past two chapters you should be able to understand that experiences are completely what you make them out to be.

You should also have a clear understanding that what people think of you really isn't relevant and that other people out there are in turn equally as terrified of what you think of them. There are much more important things in life than what people think!

12 MINUTES FOR CREATING AN ANCHOR OF CONFIDENCE

What is an "anchor"?

An **anchor** is a LEARNED association between a specific state and a specific trigger.

How are anchors created?

An anchor is created anytime you are in an INTENSE state, fully associated, with the whole body involved.

If someone **CONSISTENTLY** does <u>anything</u> **UNIQUE** at the **PEAK** of that experience, whatever they do that's unique will get **LINKED** to that state.

The Four Key Elements of Anchoring:

1. The INTENSITY of the state
2. The TIMING of the anchor
3. The UNIQUENESS of the stimulus
4. Replicating the anchor effectively

Condition yourself to feel the way you want on a consistent basis.

Anchors exist around you all the time. You simply need to be aware of them (you're always "anchoring" – your brain is making associations constantly).

Advertisers anchor us by linking certain pleasurable emotions to their products and then condition us to believe/feel this connection by <u>repetition</u>.

See how *you* can take advantage of anchors around you (music, pictures, sunshine, comedies, memories…) to create feelings of pleasure every moment of your life!

EXERCISE XI

Create a "TOTAL SELF-CONFIDENCE" anchor.

You can anchor yourself to *anything* – being happy, excited, creative, humorous, confident, or passionate…

Choose the emotion of "Being Unstoppable" … then anchor it in.

Get yourself back to times when you felt that way. Go back to the state you were in… confident, happy, motivated, excited, joyful, passionate…

Snap yourself into a confident state! Whip yourself into a passionate frenzy! Be outrageous!

MOVE your body dynamically! Jump up and down!

Think of times when you felt unstoppable!

Think of times when you were completely happy!

Imagine/visualise yourself as the person you are committed to being! Get inspired! Your Ultimate Self! The kind of self you want to keep moving towards!

Visualise/Imagine yourself being and having all the things you ever wanted!

FEEL IT!

GET EXCITED!

Right **at the peak** of the emotion, do something unique, with deep emotion! Link this state/feeling to something UNIQUE such as clicking your fingers a certain way, squeezing your shoulder while shouting "Yes", clapping your hands confidently, etc.

Then... REPEAT THIS WHOLE EXERCISE UNTIL YOU HAVE <u>CONDITIONED</u> THIS ANCHOR IN! *(Do it 12-24 times)*

Create all these buttons for your brain so that NOW, <u>YOU</u> ARE IN CONTROL!

There is TREMENDOUS power in this!

RECAP

By the end of this chapter you should be able to create an anchor of confidence for yourself and know how to practise helping your anchor secure your everyday life situations.

12 MINUTES FOR LETTING GO OF INAUTHENTIC FEARS

If you recall, at the beginning of this course we mentioned that we are born fearless — apart from the fear of falling and the fear of loud noises.

Any fear you have has been culturally programmed into you by society and your environment! They don't exist outside of your head!

These fears are utterly destructive because they stop you from going after your dreams.

They make you lead a 'small' life.

Now, fear is not all that bad. In fact, it's a very useful and powerful tool. In dangerous, life-threatening situations, it gives us deep access to our resources by creating a huge bio-chemical reaction in our body (adrenaline is pumped throughout our body).

Fear is nothing but an emotional state in which our brain tries to make us avoid *pain*.

Having said that, how many times did you feel fear, anxiety, concern... and nothing actually happened?

I'd say that 9 times out of 10 my fears have not materialized.

That means that 9 times out of 10 those were INAUTHENTIC FEARS!

You need to have a conversation with your brain. Be playful with it.

"Listen, Brain, I appreciate what you're trying to do for me here, but if I don't change jobs... if I don't go over and talk to that guy... if I don't start my own business... if I don't become successful... well, I'll miss out on x, y, z! And I won't fulfil my destiny! And that will mean ULTIMATE pain!"

If you want to be afraid about anything... BE AFRAID OF MISSING OUT ON LIFE AND NOT REALIZING YOUR DREAMS!

OVERCOMING THE FEAR OF CHANGE AND OF THE UNKNOWN

Be adventurous! Live life to the full! Try out EVERYTHING! Seek out new experiences!

Create a new belief (table-top) that says: *"Change Is Fun and Easy!"*

You see, all the juice of life, all the excitement, all the joy and passion... lies in the realm of uncertainty – The Unknown.

It makes sense, doesn't it? What is *certain* for you, is what you already know; what you already experience in your life; the tried and tested; the routine.

But all the great things that you *want* for yourself and your life, all of your dreams and aspirations, *have* to be in the realm of the unknown because they haven't occurred yet!

OVERCOMING THE FEAR OF SUCCESS

A lot of women associate pain with success. They even fear it.

They feel, "People might not like me anymore if I'm successful...", "I will lose all my friends..."

"What will happen if I can't continue succeeding?"

Also, if they've never experienced 'Success' before, it's an unknown space for them to be in (again, fear of the unknown).

To overcome this, you need to write down and focus on all the *pain* you will experience if you're *NOT* successful in life, and also on all the pleasure that success will bring you.

People will look up to you and respect you more. You will be an inspiration to them. You will have more money to do all the things you've always wanted to do, and you will never have to worry about the bills again.

OVERCOMING THE FEAR OF FAILURE

Fear of failure stops many people from going after what they really want. People tend to dwell on the *pain* they might feel if they fail.

There is no such thing as 'failure'!!! EVER!

It is absolutely IMPOSSIBLE to fail. As long as you've learned something, you have succeeded!

Trial and error is how we learn!

There is no 'failure' — only *results*! And guess what. Take enough swings at the bat, and it's inevitable that you'll hit something in the end!

Once you've been knocked down, all that matters is HOW FAST CAN YOU GET BACK UP!

Failure is impossible! You need to *tell* yourself that you've failed. Only YOU determine whether you've failed or not.

Who determines whether you're successful or not?

You and your rules.

Most people set themselves up in such a way that no matter WHAT they do they are *"failures"*.

What would *you* do with your life if you knew you could not fail?

OVERCOMING THE FEAR OF REJECTION

As with the fear of failure, the fear of rejection stops many women from going after what they want.

We're afraid of being rejected, because rejection would confirm our darkest, scariest, most crippling thoughts about ourselves... *that we're not good enough, that there's something wrong with us, that we don't deserve to be loved...*

Imagine that an idea of yours has been shot down. You need to adopt the following rules:

"MASSIVE REJECTION IS THE PATH TO SUCCESS!"

"The time isn't right, yet."

"These people are not the right people to share this with, at this time."

"Everyone has got a different view on things."

"I only need a 'yes' from that 1 right person to become a massive success."

Listen, anyone who has ever succeeded has had to face massive rejection. The TV show "M.A.S.H." was rejected by 32 studios! Sylvester Stallone was turned down by 1,000 agents!

You're going to get more rejection than acceptance. All you need is that ONE *'Yes'*...

Don't let the rejection get to you emotionally – it is just someone else's opinion.

If you're NOT getting massive rejection right now... it simply means you're playing too small a game!

Go out there and get rejected some more!

Before going into a situation where you are requesting or proposing something, use the anchoring exercise above and trigger off your anchors to make yourself feel absolutely unstoppable and strong!

Finally, to completely get over this fear, get leverage over yourself.

Ask yourself – what has been the cost in your life, of being afraid of rejection? What have you missed out on, and what will you *continue* to miss out on? How many great people are you not going to meet because of this fear? How many business opportunities will you fail to take advantage of? How many times will you feel disappointed with yourself for not having the courage to do what you know is right?

On the other hand, what are all the benefits and all the pleasure you will get from no longer being afraid of 'rejection'? How freeing will it be to no longer be concerned with what other people think of you and just go for what you want? How much joy and success will that create in your life?

RECAP

By the end of this chapter you should know that all of the fears inside of you have been conditioned into you by either society or your environment and as a result are INAUTHENTIC fears.

You should now be adequately equipped with the knowledge to:

-Overcome the fear of change and the unknown
-Overcome the fear of success
-Overcome the fear of failure
-Overcome the fear of rejection

CONFIDENCE FOR WOMEN

IT ALL COMES DOWN TO THIS (THE BIGGER PICTURE)

Play it big, take charge of your dreams and enjoy this ride we call life.

LISTEN, YOU ARE GOING TO DIE ANYWAY, SO YOU MIGHT AS WELL GO FOR IT!

BE A PLAYER IN THE GAME OF LIFE! PLAY FULL OUT! BE FULLY ALIVE! TAKE ADVANTAGE OF EVERY MOMENT YOU ARE GIVEN!

LIVE A BIG LIFE! CREATE A BIG GAME WHERE YOU ARE CHALLENGED EVERY MOMENT TO BE AT YOUR VERY BEST!

LIFE IS NOT LIKE A MOVIE... YOU ONLY GET ONE TAKE.

"Somebody should tell us right at the start of our lives that we are dying...
Then, we might live life to the limit! Every minute of every day! DO IT, I SAY! WHATEVER IT IS YOU WANT TO DO! Do it NOW!

There are only so many tomorrows..."

– Actor Michael Landon afflicted with terminal pancreatic cancer, in a 1991 Life Magazine interview.

What do you REALLY love doing? What truly fires you up? What do you want to create?

Remember, anything you can conceive, you can achieve.

FOCUS ON HELPING OTHERS.

If the #1 most important secret to achieving Total Self-Confidence is TAKING ACTION, the #2 most important secret is this: decide to focus on how you can help OTHER people achieve what THEY want.

How can you add value to their lives? How can you care for others? Who out there really *needs* you?

Focusing too much on yourself and not enough on others *guarantees* you'll lack confidence! Focus on others and contribute to other people! Stop analysing and picking yourself apart!

Trust me, if you were to ever get conscious of how the world is burning, you would stop focusing on your petty little issues, worries, anxieties. You've really got bigger fish to fry.

When you focus on giving, you are spiritual. Give your time, give your love.... You'll then *know* what you are made for. You'll then know that you are here to give, not to get.

When you live in your heart, you don't live so much in your head.

You are actually replacing FEAR... with LOVE!

Your head is where reside envy, jealousy, greed, the need for approval, the need to impress others, and low self-esteem...

Whereas in your 'heart' resides only love, passion, purpose, and truth.

You see, your head (brain) is a fear-based mechanism designed to make you survive. It isn't designed to make you happy or fulfilled. In order to make sure you survive, it will bring to your attention and magnify ANY little worry or concern that might pop up.

Whenever you experience fear, the focus is always on *you*. The fear is always about *you*.

This might seem hard to understand right now, but **the Universe rewards those that are living their lives ON PURPOSE and are serving others.** In fact, the *more* you serve others, the more you will receive back.

If you want to live your life on purpose and experience a massive shift in your quality of life, try eliminating the mantra *"What's in it for me?"* and choose instead *"How Can I Serve More People?"*

Without helping other people... you are not 'connected'. Only when you are 'connected' to the Universe will you find true fulfilment.

By the way, human beings will do more for someone they love than they would ever do for themselves. Who do you care about so much that you will devote your life to making theirs better? What causes do you really believe in and would like to support? Find a team of people you would do anything for. This will drive you and keep you focused.

QUIT WORKING TOO HARD AND LIVE YOUR PURPOSE

How do you survive in a world where "There's something wrong with me... I'm not good enough..."?

Well, you become determined to make it! You work hard until you succeed! You strive to "look good". You strive to be admired by other people. You act sincere, well-meaning... "Nice".

It's all a sham to cover up "There's something wrong with me... I'm not good enough..."

You hope to fake it long enough so that people don't discover that... *"There's something wrong with me... I'm not good enough..."*

It's all absurd!

There's nothing wrong with you, and who you are is simply magnificent!

Many people work very hard to achieve success only to find that when they do they still feel inadequate, as if underneath their achievements they stand as an impostor. Success keeps the wolf away from the door for about 30 seconds. *"I've made it and I'm STILL not good enough! WHEN WILL IT END?!!"*

Success will never make you fulfilled. You *want* to succeed because deep inside... *"I'M NOT GOOD ENOUGH!"*

You're no good, there's something wrong with you, you don't belong... so you *"work hard",* in the hope that if you suffer enough people will like you.

"Wow, you've really suffered, how honourable..."

And then BOOM, you're dead.

All this is disgusting behaviour, because it is so utterly inauthentic! It is completely out of integrity with who you really are and what you are really here to do!

YOU CAN'T EVEN TELL THE TRUTH TO PEOPLE! THAT'S APPALLING! YOU STARTED OUT AS "ANYTHING IS POSSIBLE!"... AND YOU'VE ENDED UP WITH THIS???!!!

Working hard is stupid! Discover your true purpose and LIVE IT! Anything that fills you up with joy is NOT hard work. You are just joyous and present in the moment.

Do you think there's any place for *"I'm not good enough"* when you are living your purpose?

Of course not! You are being fully alive!

DISCOVER YOUR PURPOSE

EXERCISE XII

To discover your purpose, ask yourself these questions:

1. What would you be doing right now, if you had absolutely no limitations, you were a billionaire, and you knew you could not fail?
2. What would you share with the world, if your message were to be broadcast throughout all of the world's television stations for 5 minutes?

BEING IN THE FLOW OF LIFE

Most extraordinarily successful people would do what they do for free – and many of these same people are outstanding at what they do. Their confidence is unshakable, and they make enormous amounts of money.

They are simply in the flow of life.

It is the actions and achievements of these people they write about in history books.

If you follow their lead, you'll appear to work harder than ever before... and yet you won't work a day in your life, and you'll be happier than ever before. You'll be calm and confident.

When work and play blend, and you don't want to go home at the end of the working day, then you know you're fulfilling your purpose in life.

When you are in the flow of life, you are passionate about what you do, excited about the future, driven, motivated, successful, enthusiastic, joyful, creative, and fully self-expressed. You are fully *alive*. You feel like you're in the right place. You are guided. It is effortless. Everything just flows. The right situations and people come to you, and it feels like you can't put a foot wrong.

What's the possibility out there that WANTS <u>YOU</u>? What is the mission that is powerfully calling <u>you</u> into being?

DISCOVER IT... AND THEN GIVE YOUR LIFE TO IT! PUT IN YOUR WHOLE HEART, YOUR WHOLE SOUL, YOUR WHOLE BEING!!!

This takes courage, integrity, and passion. But TAKE A STAND FOR WHAT YOU BELIEVE IN!

A stand is unreasonable. It's ferocious when it has to be. When you take a stand, you cannot be moved. You are bold and unreasonable.

Remember that on your deathbed, you will never wish you'd spent more time in the office...

Do what you LOVE in life! Close your eyes and picture yourself at your perfect job. Can you see it? What are you doing? Don't ever settle for where you are if it is incongruent with what you really want to be doing.

"If money was no object and you knew you could not fail, what would you do in your life?" - The immediate answer to this question will uncover your passion and what you should be doing right now.

Have you ever done a completely selfless act, and helped someone out of the goodness of your heart?

Didn't it feel AMAZING?

I would like you to consider for a second the possibility that THAT is what we are all here for.

We all share the same PURPOSE, and yet it is different for each and every one of us.

We get to express it in our own, unique way, with our specific talents and abilities.

If we are truly – as a lot of spiritually enlightened people have said – spirits having a human experience here on Earth, with the purpose of expressing LOVE and contributing to our fellow man, wouldn't it stand to reason that when we put our life ON PURPOSE, we find ourselves? It's like coming home. We find 'balance': inner peace.

SPIRITUAL ENLIGHTENMENT AND TOTAL SELF-CONFIDENCE

In a series of books by Lee Carroll, the author channels the spiritual entity 'Kryon' (www.kryon.com).

According to Kryon, he is one of many spiritual entities who are of service to Mankind, doing the work of God, from the other side of the 'veil'.

He explains that we are in fact spiritual beings having a human experience – we are *'in lesson'* here in this *'school'* called Earth, for the purpose of growing our awareness and thus raising our vibration by getting more and more enlightened through expressing more love, peace, and tolerance.

This process is critical in the grand scheme of things because it transmutes negativity throughout the Universe.

Kryon mentions that Jesus is one of the highest vibrations in the Universe, one of the highest ascended masters ever to visit the Earth, and was sent to us to teach us about truth and love.

Because we, as spiritual entities, have elected to suffer and die over and over again for the good of the whole, we are loved beyond measure by all entities in the Universe. We are the exalted ones.

We each have 2 spirit guides that communicate with us through our intuition and our dreams. Kryon advises us to communicate with them through prayers, asking out loud what we need.

Apparently, they MUST respond.

According to Kryon, each of us is a part of God – there is a part of us that has been around for trillions of years... forever, in fact.

This means that we are all part of the same ONE consciousness.

If there's any truth to any of this, if indeed we are all part of the same BEING, surely the only feeling one should experience is... Love?

Love for everything and everyone, for they are part of us and we a part of them.

So it's quite funny when we judge other people, or fear *their* judgement, fear what they think about us, try to be better than others, compete with others, go to war against and kill others, or argue and fight with each other...

Listen, every human being has been put here for a reason. You are way more important than you know.

What does this mean for your sense of self-confidence?

Know that there is a timeless place inside of you that has unlimited and eternal love that you can tap into at any time. Nurture this gift within yourself so that you may have more to give.

The truth is you will feel loved any time you love, any time you cherish yourself, value life, value nature, or value others...any time you express love.

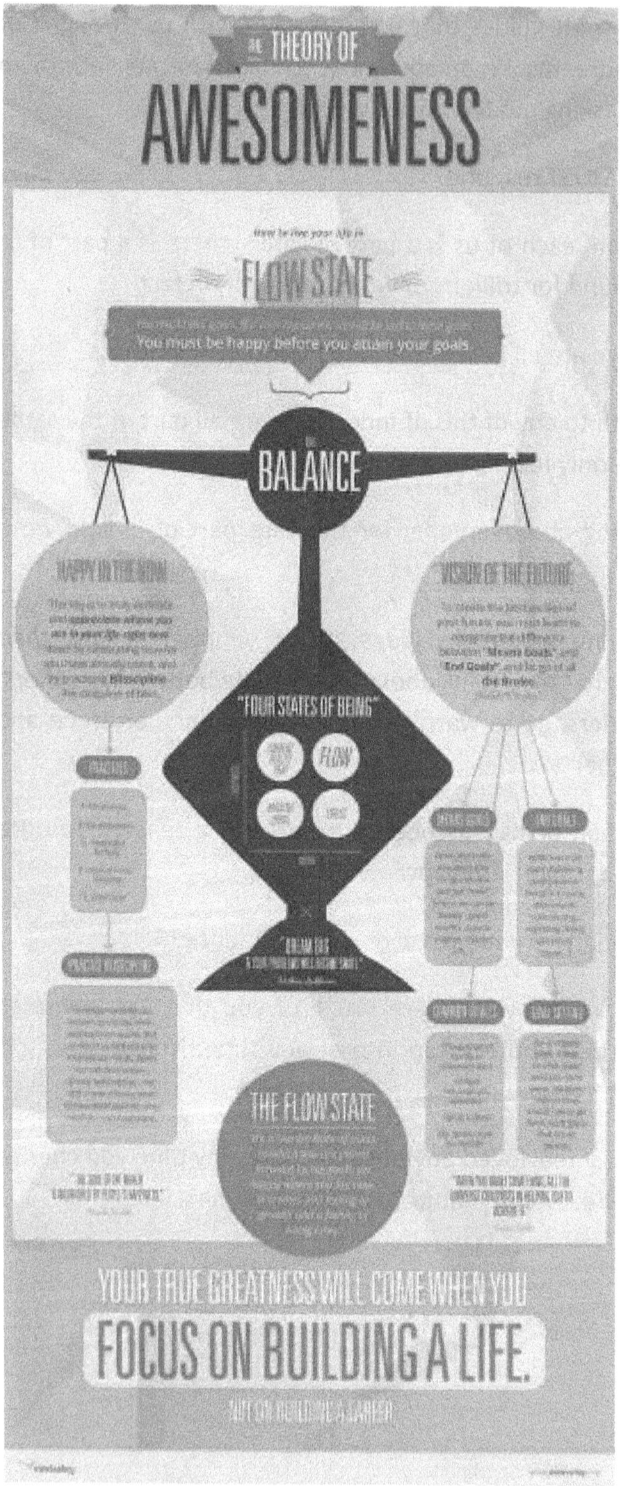
THEORY OF
AWESOMENESS
FLOW STATE
You must be happy before you attain your goals
BALANCE
HAPPY IN THE NOW
VISION OF THE FUTURE
"FOUR STATES OF BEING"
THE FLOW STATE
YOUR TRUE GREATNESS WILL COME WHEN YOU
FOCUS ON BUILDING A LIFE.

CONFIDENCE FOR WOMEN

THE TOTAL RECAP

1 BUY A JOURNAL & PRACTICE SELF ANALYSIS

-What is there in your life that you are not happy about? How can you change this?

-What are 2 realities about yourself you find difficult to accept completely?

-When do you feel the most angry or frustrated?

-List 5 fears you currently hold. What do you fear most in your life right now? Why?

-Complete the following beginnings:

-'I like myself least when I...'

-'I like myself most when I...'

2 BE TOTALLY HONEST WITH YOURSELF

-Admit what your flaws are.

-Take ownership of your feelings.

-Release the guilt over things you keep bottled up inside.

-Who has wronged you in the past?

-Whom have *you* wronged in the past?

-With whom do you need to "complete" with so that neither of you carry this issue around anymore? (Make a list)

-Write them a letter explaining what was going on for you, and how you feel about it now. You don't *need* to be apologetic – although people are bowled over when someone has the courage and self-esteem to admit they were wrong – you can simply acknowledge what happened for you.

-Contact them by phone and read the letter out to them.

3 BUILDING YOUR DREAM OUTCOME

-Imagine that you were granted 1 wish – what would you dare to dream, if you knew you could not fail?

-What kind of work would you truly enjoy and be passionate about?

-Where do you want to travel? What would you want to experience?

-If you only had 6 months to live, what would you do with that remaining time?

-What knowledge or skill would you like to acquire?

-What do you want for your body and your health?

-What do you want to achieve financially?

-What would you like buy? What have you always wanted to buy?

-What specific characteristics do you want your ideal life partner to possess?

-What would you like to contribute to the world? What would you like to create?

-What would your dream house look like? What would be in it?

-Who are your heroes? Who would you like to be more like?

-What character traits would you like to develop? What would your *Code of Conduct* be?

4 APPRECIATION AND THANKSGIVING

Now that you've written down your goals, your Code of Conduct, your Board of Directors, your compelling future and your Life Script... VISUALIZE THEM! Play a mental movie in your head, and then see yourself *in* that movie!

5 POSITIVE AFFIRMATION

Create a sentence to describe yourself such as "I am an Outstanding, Inspirational, and Charismatic Leader and Visionary, that Makes a Difference and Defies All Odds!"

6 DEVOTION AND DISCIPLINE – COMMITTING TO THE CAUSE

-Write down your own "Power Regimen" – what are *you* committed to doing every day?

-Commit to being self-confident and sticking to what you want to achieve in life EVERY SINGLE DAY!

7 BE REAL

-Just say NO.

-Never cave in and conform.

8 MEANINGFUL MIND CONTROL

-All that you are is a result of what you have thought.

-What are you grateful for in life?

-What are you really excited about right now?

-Who do you love and who really loves you?

(Read your answers frequently every day, with *feeling*).

9 SEE THINGS THE WAY THEY ARE

-Experiences in our lives have no meaning other than what we attach to them.

-You have the power to choose how you perceive a situation.

-What events in your life have been blown totally out of proportion?

-What meanings did you attach to those events?

10 DON'T CARE ABOUT WHAT "THEY" THINK

-99% of what people do is about "looking good" in fear of "what others will think of them."

-99% of people out there are terrified of what YOU think of THEM.

11 CREATE A POWERFUL TOTAL SELF-CONFIDENCE 'ANCHOR'!

-Get yourself back to times when you felt totally confident. Think of times when you felt unstoppable! *Feel* the state you were in ...confident, happy, motivated, excited, joyful, and passionate...

-Snap yourself into a passionate, totally confident state! Whip yourself into a passionate frenzy! Be outrageous! MOVE your body! Run! Jump up and down!

-Imagine and visualise yourself as the person you are committed to being! Get inspired! Your - Ultimate Self! The kind of self you want to keep moving towards!

-Visualise/Imagine yourself being and having all the things you ever wanted!

-*FEEL* IT! GET EXCITED!

-Right at the PEAK of the emotion, do something unique, with deep emotion! You need to link this state/feeling to something UNIQUE such as clicking your fingers a certain way, or shouting "Yes" whilst clapping your hands confidently.

-Then... REPEAT THIS WHOLE EXERCISE UNTIL YOU HAVE CONDITIONED THIS ANCHOR IN! *(Do this 12-24 times).*

12 LET GO OF INAUTHENTIC FEARS

-Fears have been culturally programmed into you by society and your environment.

-Fears make you lead a small life.

-Never let the fear of failure keep you from living to the fullest.

-Overcoming the Fear of the Unknown

-Overcoming the Fear of Success

CONFIDENCE FOR WOMEN

-Overcoming the Fear of Failure

-Overcoming the Fear of Rejection

FINAL THOUGHTS

This concludes the course of *"The Total Twelve – Your 12 Step Plan for Total Confidence as a Woman Making Your Own Way."* I sincerely hope that you have enjoyed reading it, and that you have already started putting the techniques I've mentioned into practice.

Masters practice the fundamentals over and over again. *DO* the exercises and you will be *amazed* at the impact this will have on your life.

I feel privileged to have had the opportunity to inspire you with my words. I wish you well on your journey.

Remember that life is for living! You *can* be unstoppable, you *can* achieve unlimited success, and you DEFINITELY *can* go after your dreams.

I'll leave you with a quote by Jim Rohn:

"Let others lead small lives, but not you.

Let others argue over small things, but not you.

Let others cry over small hurts, but not you.

Let others leave their future in someone else's hands, but not you."

www.ingramcontent.com/pod-product-compliance
Lightning Source LLC
Chambersburg PA
CBHW071456070426
42452CB00040B/1546